DUMPSTERFIRE PRESS
(GRAND RAPIDS, MI)
USA

Cover art by "Ending" James Maj

 Cover design by Mike Zone

Edited by Mike Zone

 ISBN: 9798408706211

Manufactured in the United States of America.

Dumpster Fire Press was founded on primarily giving voices to the voiceless and that's extended beyond Central and Northern America and all across a multitude of spectrums.

From China, Portugal, Germany, Nepal, Kurdistan, South America, Israel, Spain, Iraq, Britain, Ireland, Ukraine and members of the LGBTQ community along with the marginalized working class we strive to give writers and artists a voice. It's one of the foundations of the **PUNK** aspect of DFP to embrace diversity, keeping an open mind to further advance knowledge of where the entirety of human culture is heading or sometimes stagnating.

It is due to these values regardless of geopolitics we present to you the work of John Chinaka Onyeche a poetic storyteller of his own making.

While we do not always have to agree on policy and spirituality, what we do agree on is poetry and storytelling from a unique perspective from a voice that needs to be heard or yearns to heard.

From out of Nigeria, we are honored to present the work of John "The Apostle" Chinaka Onyeche in the hopes the reader will learn, further the actions of contemplation and explore vast terrain of what can be perceived as beauty.

Now let's start a revolution!
Joking...sort of...

Mike Zone

Echoes Across the Atlantic

By

John Chinaka Onyeche

Dedication

This book is dedicated to Rev Father Kelvin Agbakolom.

To my lovely wife (Ezigbom) Ogechukwu Brigid.

To the strength of my youth Chidebem Sobeife.

To Mr Thank God Iruegbo.

To my siblings, Chiemena, Ikechi and Ruth.

To Mummy Pst Mrs. Margaret Umukoro.

To Mike Zone.

FORWARD

We could be hard on ourselves at times, always pointing out the features we liked least about ourselves. We'd always agree that there were periods of time when we felt we were really good and then others where we just thought it wasn't worth it – as though our joy took a vacation and some stranger replaced it with foreign gloom. As much as we switched up positive vibes or put up happy faces, during those down times, there was not much we could do to make us like how life treats us. Life has its ups and downs. When you are up, enjoy the scenery. When you are down, touch the soul of your being and feel the beauty.

In John Chinaka Onyeche's *Echoes Across The Atlantic*, you will learn that there are always going to be weird times, whether it's with your physical appearances or your emotional and mental state; there is always going to be the swing swaying back and forth. The difference between the ups and downs is that you are not just grasping at the ropes of the swing, trying to hang on, rather, you are propelling your legs to direct it. In other words, you can be in charge of your life's echoes. If you can promise that you will believe in the uniqueness of your contribution, that you will trust in what you know you are capable of, then you will dance on the Atlantic to the tunes of life's echoes until the shores of 'end' come calling.

You will come to embrace the swing and welcome the turbulence of the ride; to not fear falling off or getting hurt. It's really easy to be fearful and judge the varying degrees of emotions housed within you, but it is harder, more rewarding work to unravel each new feeling as though it were a gift delivered to you at exactly the right time.

John Chinaka Onyeche, with his collection of poems would show you in vivid verses how your life is not about pushing away the uncomfortable, the scary, the messy, or the weird, but rather trying to discover what purpose they have for you in your life. We're never going to be able to control the ebbs and flows that current through our journeys, but we can learn to love the aspects of ourselves that we normally like to run from.

Life is like a swing - it has thrilling ups and it has depressing downs. But life isn't about the exact quantity of ups and downs, but rather how smoothly we ride between these inevitable ups and downs, and that is what 'Echoes Across The Atlantic' is about.

Writing this foreword has been a great honour for me and I believe that this book in your hand will throw the same feeling at you. May these poems birth ideas, and may they multiply thoughts. Happy reading.

Jaachị Ányátọnwụ
Author, Diary of a Broken Poet

The Lady In Red

To the last lady in red,
the one who watches me, -
from the windowpane,
of the old city mansion.

You have vowed to be -
my letch daily; on - sticks -
of loneliness, and many,
a heart fervor, for you.

Your thighs would welcome,
the lost soul to the kingdom, -
the one not built with hands,
of men of this world, -

But you have chosen daily,
to be my murderer in wants,
and have so chosen to burn me
with these - unquenchable fires.

Of my longings in a land filled with, -
the drought of love and my flames of -
desiring you burn to infinity,
as I long each day to be with you.

Oh, come in with your eminent waters,

come to my rescue in this land of,

drought and loneliness of heart,

and make me feel the paradise within.

MY FATHER WORE GRIEF AS A GARMENT.

Today my father cuts his hair low,
he looks older & tired.
i can see it from his eyes,
myriad of life's untold tales.

i am looking through his private diaries locked up & hidden,
maybe i will be lucky to see some o good, recorded memories
of himself on what life was like to him while growing up.

there is this big box full of Bibles,
from where he wrote our names, -
with each passage, our names are engraved -
and special prayer points attached to it.

he had brought this box to my mother as a gift,
when they both settled their last quarrel, -
which i believe he holds it dear to this Bible and box,
as they lived the rest of their lives separated.

when i reckon of how much i have been through,
i think of how much my father has lived to endure
as the result of the ill felted marriage with my mother,
as all i could see written on his face are scares of grief.

I doubt it if god knows how much

9

my father has been able to endure within himself,

everyday remembrance of us, - hands him over to grief;

& he evaporates like mist each without our knowledge.

today, my father cuts his hair low to mourn

his ill felted marriage with my mother

& his grief, he wore as a garment.

Boys Are Not Stones

This is how they cracked us away from each other,
& caved us into the stones that we are never one -

Yesterday, I took a walk into the house of a curator,
The one who makes good use of woods to create,
Of the things in the unseen images of his heart,
& the magnificence in the eyes of its beholder.

As he laid down a tablet of stone & named it - boys; -
& I watched him chisel intercepting lines on the stone;
On each line, he whispered to my ears myriad of names,
Of boys whom he had known, & who have become like,

A breezy day in the month of their nightmares -
How they journeyed into time and waves of life, -boys; -
Echoes of many unfulfilled dreams and longings,
This story was about boys who are not stones -
At the threshold of his masterful drawing board,
He cracked the names of the boys in time's archives.

The Spot

Each night I dance,

in the same rhythm

we have made our ritual,

I look out as the moon

and the stars through

the windowpane,

from the same spot

we had stood million times.

To watch the stars dance

in the orbit of the night skies,

just as we have become like them

in a million ways;

and this spot at our altars of rituals,

I stand here tonight,

with a million burnt thoughts, -

erecting habitats for our memories,

I am beginning to fall ill for nostalgia

where we make our rituals daily,

at the altar as the stars in their orbits dance

for the songs we sing,

they are eternal velocity

that words can't be utter.

For Boys Like Me

We are like a page in a book,

But, blank for time & history,

to be written on.

Just as my mother had told me -

in her last days;

boys are like trees.

In boys, we have logs,

each sawed outright,

but with time to be transformed -

Into materials of crafting,

most we write our stories with,

& our histories about life.

How it has been with us,

a journey, a must-survival, -

but, - it is said that;

boys are not stones,

for stones are picked up,

from their calling -

& we placed them,

where they don't belong,

to roll into many unknown holes of life,

they rolled seeking to withstand -

the kicks of life as many are cast-off -

13

as wounded in their verve.

When Love First Found Us.

When love first found us, // we became like a broken mirror; // who's pieces twinkles like diamonds, // even in its gloomy days; // it chooses to shine in its entirety; // For over its quandary of the journey, // it held up its lights of reflectivity; // of what it means to be a mirror, // it stood out more and become. // the question is; have you seen a broken man, // he shades off his many grieves // & reflect well in painstaking, // of what life has been like to him, // he lives each day remolding himself; // because he never stops believing. // Have you seen a virgin; // one who lost her lover, // in the eve of their wedding; // she floods her heavens, // with rivers of flowing agonies, // from the forest of brokenness; // and wilderness of shattered dreams, // where dwells no living, // and of that uninhabitable kingdom of longings, // with which she dies each night; // never desiring to live the next day for life had dealt with her. // This was our voyage when love first found us and broke our hearts.

Insomnia

Yesterday, I could not find my siesta, -

as I have heard that she helps, -

to ameliorate a man's days stress.

& my eyebrows promenade Fuji, -

all night long as my body joined,

I couldn't find the lover of my eyes.

as she had tendered her lover - a divorce letters, -

for the week past I have resolved within me; -

Going to see a surgeon - maybe.

to help me & manage this damage,

the once caused by her letter;

which has evoked me with trauma.

For You

I am becoming a watchman

To watch over your inks that flow into tiny air

For you,

I am becoming an African

From the Southern tip of Africa

For you,

I am becoming the first inhabitant of the Cape

For you,

I am becoming the first owner of the land

For you,

I am becoming the first race known as the San

For you,

I will go with my bands into the forest and pick wide berries

For you,

I have become the hunter and gatherers

For you,

We will go into the mountains and pick pebbles

Each man on his bands, we will gather up stones

For you,

We will return to use the stones to make you a grave

For you died a hero in the land of your so journal

For you,

We will use our stones to build you a grave,

THOUGHTS

I was invaded by the memories
Of the past that I had wished not mine;
Just like a city without a wall, it crept in,
With arms to render asunder.

It was on a turbulent eve of circs,
Where solitude was akin to a graveyard,
& I reached out to the mountain to hold:
But it becomes like a speck of dust and vanishes.

Like the turbulence that cascades,
I wandered away from this house;
As the memories of the past expanses;
The more my invaders are armed.

With every single mistake made,
My walls of defense lay down low;
Just like a city without a defense lay,
So my thoughts about yesterday laid.

In the hands of thought that invades a man,
So I lay, pondering about the name life:
Life on earth, what does it have for men and women?

As A Nation

With the cranky noise of guns, -
And booming sounds of bombs; -
Without our Pan-Africanist goals:
We have become more wars, -
More we have not become peace.

A nation under one name,
A nation under one God,
A nation under one heaven:
A nation under one earth,

With the cranky noise of guns, -
And booming sounds of bombs; -
While disunity uproot our roots, -
We have become more battles; -
More we have not become stability.

This is who we are as a Nigerians,
This is the story we shall tell our kids;
This is where our leaders has dumped us;
In a dungeon of hatred and nepotism.

Village People

We have made our way to the caves.

When we had decided to run from our nests
into the dark caves for the safety of our lives -
Men and women thought us to be cowards -
As the street and states weren't home again
We embrace the rascality of the dense forest

To survive our race to the next generation of men -
We have been hunted down even by our own men -
As hands we had once bent low to feed their mouths
In the time past and favourable moments of ours -

They now lay their fist against our - guts - that breath
they seek annihilation in a house full of life
and our wings became like that of an eagle bird -

And to the top mountains of land with zeal, we have flown
not to return as preys to be devoured by hands
not even the filthy hands of men from this earth

Africa, Seen As A Cave Of Darkness

"The Chinaman meets you with the stolid morality of his Confucianism; the Hindoo with astute logic for his pantheism... When I carry my touch into the caves of Africa, I meet only filthy birds of darkness." Returned Missionary 1873.

History is biased to my continent, -

and only the few of us would tell; -

how it is in every race stood culture, -

some to the human detrimental; -

and others to their development. -

But why is my Africa is likened to men in caves, -

while her development and culture; -

with men across the sea is seen as evil, -

even that which happens in their lands. -

History is prejudice to the black man, -

it tells of my origin in another's tongue; -

wrecking me my pride and sense of belonging; -

to the human families to which I belongs. -

Histories of the blacks are told with one-sidedness; -

with the mind-set of dehumanizing his race, -

this is another way history prejudices, -

of the people of our African descent.

Caves of darkness; where raw materials; -

they sourced from; in their quest to rule, -

a land where their gods has kept their golds; -

maybe for their invasion and conquest.

Within their mouths, the streets of Bini is never mentioned, -

where the inhabitants of the great city lights; -

up their city entrance to the kingdom with palm-oil, -

because it is not in their language to write; -

of our mind bewildering craftsmanship. -

In their quest to write about us the men's of Africa,

they were so - occupied by negative notions of race,-

as my Africa is seen as a cave of darkness and not

as a continent.

IN MY COUNTRY,

In my country, death wears the faces of our favorite masquerade
and dances before our eyes as good omens.

Who would have believe that we once fought together -

against the one whom we dubbed our common enemy,

the forces at will, - the heartlessness as colonialism,

tooth and nail we demanded for the freedom to rule, -

rule ourselves as a people and a state of nations -

we became lawlessness in the quest for freedom,

as freedom became our only voice heard abroad -

but how have we allowed freedom to elude us -

slaying the same voice that echoed liberty at dawn. -

In my country, death wears the faces of our politicians and
dances before our eyes as good omens.

Because we have become much more of nepotism, - leaving the
wounded soul of patriotism at birth,

where we had prevailed over sledgehammer of time -

and rehabilitate ill politics by the blood of passer-by

of those who once were thrilled by the masquerade -

the one who dances before our very own eyes - not -

as omens, but as a real one that we all wanted to watch,

as a nation - under one name, one earth and one God.

In my country, death wears the faces of our favorite masquerade
and dances before our eyes as good omens.

We have been taught never to feel pains of sudden death,

of those who stood out to defend the liberty we have, -

those whose voice would have been heard for good,

that their ends comes in seconds for the fear of losing, -

the seats of political power and office of influence,

we laugh and cry for the things that we should rejoice in

watching the masquerade made away with lives of those, -

who standby to watch and to cheer it up for displaying, -

we call it development by the blood of every citizens.

In my country, death wears the faces of our politicians and
dances before our eyes as good omens.

It invades us with mouth-watering promises from birth, -

and leaves us with heart-wrenching doubt of surviving, -

in the hands of fear to live or rejoice to die away from earth, -

with every terror it attacks us with each day and night,-

as day-to-day lives of the citizens are mashed up, -

by terror or hardship to live the next day of their lives, -

the government regulates who lives and who doesn't, -

even those who we run to for survival runs too for fears of death.

Farewell To Our Sorrow

Our grief for yesteryear's ills
Today it has on-board the ship
Sailing across the country's seas
Formed by tears of our forefathers
As none wishes to hold the ship back
Sorrows and slavery fare thee well
We are children of the black race
The book of history hold us dear
We belong with the brightness of life
Of our land and the waters it holds
At the cradle of this invented man
We are existing and have existed
At this waterway of our existence
Created by the tears of Africans
As the quest for the life of others
Men across our tears in rejoice
Let the same tears be shipped
Tonight as we gathered here
To bid farewell to our sorrows

Count Your Blessings

Before we amble into the aisle,
And the bells tolling in raging order,
Fifteen-eight-twenty-twenty-one;
There was a whisper within me,
It says, take up your quipu device,
With every string-like line;
And each cord in distinct colours,
Marked with knots of memories,
Read the meaning to their ears,
What episodes life amasses you.

At the threshold of life's scenes,
We have become men in boys shadow,
Kissing every hurricane of memories;
Of course, those who swallowcd up;
Our goals in a broad spectrum of time,
And left us as a wounded lion in the jungle,
Nonetheless, we have prevailed over it,
Our bells tolling to the adulthood of esprit.

Our bruises are buried in a nutshell of times,
As time heals all the wounded lions of the jungle;
Yes, we have withstood the raging waters of life,
And over the high hills of life's hope cheers;

There the echoes of accolades are heard of,

As we ascended to the life's hills in numbers;

Fifteen-eight-twenty-twenty-one;

The voice whispered again, this time,

Count your blessings and name them,

One by one.

1441

The indefinite that became definite,
You could have looked for a way out.
Bringing with you to my ancestors,
Good news instead of humiliations.
You are a curse to events of time alas!

Antam, you who hunted to and fro,
The sea lions in the souls of kinsmen,
You hunted them like a good hunter,
As they valued labouring as the oil,
And their blood on the vessels cries,
Africa has hunted as sea lions ashore.

Rio de Oro the land where stood first,
Prester John the legendary priest of Africa,
At your name, men were captured alas!
Looked upon to see if they could find you,
Men presented to you oh! Prince Henry,
For we understand humanity at heart,
You rather have chosen to raid and enslave us,
Quest for the annihilation of a people.

1434, the footsteps are seen at the shore,
They were not the lion skins you seek,

but of my kinsmen's backs you are torn,

1441 the blood of my ancestors' dirge

Flowing at the Atlantic Ocean red

They wore not the oil of the sea lions

Their gold in your quest you made them cry

Voyage Of Love

Such lovely words,
you spoke to my ears
that unfolds my heart
like petals of a rose

I am regained in you
& we are complete
unbroken chords

Take me tonight
to that lost kingdom
let's make our beds
in every rose petals
leaving none broken
upon this rose beds

Underneath this tree
come again and speak
please those words
the ones you spoke
at the beginning of this
voyage of love in Tokyo

Do The gods Sleep In Our Plights

To those beautiful souls long forgotten
and to those souls who irrigated our deserts
To the ones who graced our history as a race
and to those great legends in our journey
To the ones who retold our African tales
even with the languages of the conquerors
And bring to the limelight our ancestors bravery
Now speak to us through the flute and the gongs
Tell us what you are like in the great beyond
and we will advance and change our course
For life hereafter your departure is fitful

To that Akara woman at the junction
The one who rises with the first cockcrow
and begin to make Akara for the inhabitants
All for her son to see the four walls of -
education
But to whose son left school for fraternity
And died as a result of one rival scuffle
Leaving the woman heartbroken and dead
For all her hard-earned money is become -
Like a bottle of oil punctured on a sunny day
To which there is no way to be scooped up
For after you left here, life has become jaws of life

To Madu the young man who angry mobs -

gathered at the market square weeks ago

Whose voice and agony the mobs overpowered

rendering him powerless to the point of death -

To which he has been a survivor in many ways

Kill him, kill him, kill him, why should he live again

He came to buy market with counterfeit notes

In a country where everything is a counterfeit

To Amaechi the only surviving daughter

The one out of the benevolence of the villagers

She was sent to the college for more education

Blessed by the gods as she harnesses talent upon talents

Are they who are blessed by the gods supposed to be -

left alone to suffer from man's cruelty

Amaechi after two months in school was raped

Raped to her death by boys in men's clothing and who

lacks the will to control the man underneath them -

and leaving us with a question to ask, where were the gods

Does it mean even the gods sleep in our plights?

Remember This Again

Tonight as I lay down my bed
On each petal and buds of roses
All I can imagine is the love
The one shared from the beginning

As I lay tonight on this garden
I long to gather up my whole being
As nothing else could be said
That our love has swirled here

With every tone flowing through
This guitar tonight as I lay behind
I long to wake up in your palace
To put up my once shattered art

At Your Death

As we gathered last night
Behind our saddened hearts
Before the distance land

Our hearts long for a home
One that is across this land
And with our gathered tears

We built you the ocean floor
That your caskets would sail
Into that beautiful Paradise

Adieu compatriot comrade
Who died when life was needed
For everyone to it fully

Fellow soldiers, tonight,

With these one thousand candles,
& this ten thousand matches
We will all match to the year 1976,

& to all those soldiers who died
& to all those innocent infants
Who could not utter a word of theirs,
But was hit by a life bullet of anger

To the voluntary soldiers &
To the mandatory fighters
To the circumstanial men of arms &
To the professional men of arms

And to those men who died in the dark,
And to those who died in the bright day
And to those who become like mist
And they fly away from our midst

Comrades, tonight,
With these candles, and flames
We will match into their tombs
And together we shall mourn them
Bent down to their graves and say

Here is your light cut short again

We Curate Our Memories In Six Days

So yesterday I have lately lost in myself

When I took up a paper and pen and painted you.

At every corner of the four walls of this room,

& I adorned it with your six favourite colours.

Black & white as I become the curator of memories,

& as I placed each one on each wall of this room.

Just as it is believed that the earth is spherical,

But we are found often with one word.

"four corners of the world"

East, West, South and North & it was amazing as I behold it.

The four pieces of your memories hang out there,

The nostalgia of what we use to know before.

All of these written boldly in our last picture,

I looked directly into those eyes and I saw,

The pains and the desire for survival in this jungle.

But there came a whispering wind from the sky,

& it immerses me with this number six.

Take up your pen and paper notwithstanding,

Curate the memories of this nostalgia in six forms.

Make for the East one, another for the West,

Take up with the North and the South.

Look up above you and behold a thousand faces,

& make one for the heavens and the other for the earth.

As we are children of heaven inhabiting the earth,

& we know that God created the world in six days,

& as we all die and be buried in a six faces box

Underneath six feet away from this noisy world's life

Let us curate our memories and time spent here in six days.

I AM

I am the Africa,

The one you called less

I am an African,

The reality you hide

I am the son of the earth

The one you walk on

I am Africa,

The land of great warriors

I am the Africa,

The shallow tales you told at the cradle

I am the black race

The source of your choice

I am the good stories, but,

The ones that you told wrongly,

I am an African

The stories, I am here to retell

If there was comfort in your land,

There was peace and tranquility within me.

If there was a civilization with you,

In that long street stretched to Bini

There stood lampstands with beaming lights

Guiding our feet against the stones

If there were any wonders with you,

In the kingdom of Egypt and Pharaohs

We have built pyramids with our hands

Laying foundation upon foundations with bricks.

If there were the gods with you,

We have built temples and shrines here.

I am the Africa,

The story that you wrongly told

I am the Africa,

The land you invade and desecrated

And I am here to retell my tales

I am here to show the world

That I am not the wrong way of the stories told

I am the Africa,

The land flowing with milk and honey

I am Africa,

The land of the great warriors

And my stories shall be retold

As I lit them and live them up to the world

Look, my friend

I will mourn you here,
in every droplet of inks
the one that drops on -
every paper on this desk

Let every drop of it tell,
your kind soul snatched
away from all of us here
how does one muffle their -
pains,

I mean, when they come
naked and hit our eggshell
forgetting its fragility
and left us in the dust of dirge

When I heard the news
about your sudden death
I cried and create with my tears
an ocean to help me sail my grief,
Away from this intersects roads -
of this painful parts of men

Symphonies

Play me a voiceless music

one from where every tones aligns

in sequence and orderliness

whispering from within echoes

songs not found in words of mouth,

but from the stillness of the soul,

the hidden part of all there's

where the pool of fountains flows

& which brings together peace

& triumphant symphonies

& return all souls to our paradise

play me every notes and chords

from this world into the bliss

for there belongs all hearts of man

Take up your light!

Light out the darkness,

At the same time as yesterday

When the darkness took hold of you

Leading your bright part into oblivion

So we shall all gathered with lights

To light out every darkness from your way

As we have seen in your works here,

They are of the light source and not darkness

Sadness

I will now open wide my mouth

to mourn you out from this end

for the heart is without words

to express its bereavement

for which your call into beyond

has left it with many painted pains

Are We Not Servile To Life?

We are drudge of life

As we are daily owed

From dusk to dawn

Our toil and moil

Most of us go

Through this life

In delinquent by life

Our little lives

But why so soon

The little bird we caught

when after our thousand toil and moil

At the little twinkle of an eyes

They flew out our hearts

Rendering us heartbroken

For we see silhouettes -

Of futures in a nutshell -

And dreams of Kingbirds

Unfulfilled in our little lives

We Live On

I am hiding in this dark end

From where your death has hidden me,

With vultures hovering over my head

As though they see beyond my soul

What sorrow your death has caused me

& longings to live seems far from me

But I have returned to our memories

Where we have lived and died in our inks

Nightfall

But with many stars -

in the constellation of

which it lighten up my alley

& make me wonder

For why do we have -

Nightfall

Last night

We all matched in street of sorrow

& to the sea we all stood afar off

As we gaze into the ocean -

of our grief and pains of life

& as the sailors showed up

They show us the part you followed

As we waited until the morning

Still your fading shadow dazzled

Into memories for which we shared

Death

Tonight I shall take a walk

into the oceans of sorrow

to see if I can find you there!

I heard that you took the last strength within you

& walked into the oblivious air!

Friends and family gathered

& looking into your smiling face

But your face only brought dirge

to those who gathered here

& and they said if death was for the sinners,

why do you have to die on this good day of your life?

Pains Of Death

I am just like a -

stagnant river,

Yes, I have my way

& my odor

Why furor me -

on this cold eve?

Don't you know -

I reek to the highest -

heavens & pour out

My dirge as a prayer.

Sadness

I will now return - to

the hooting songs of an owls,

For the winter rain that rained today,

It has cracked the eggshell

& taking away that which -

makes me beautiful

Water And Waste

In the wake of the day

men became bedlam

as the result of hunger

the satiety for owning it all

& the quest to acquire it all

At all cost, men asleep

& as at will and all costs

There are lives like waters,

but inside the seek for gold

Like the cup, we are fixed into

At the glance of my value

Men from this other side

They began rushing to us

As we are thrown out

And our lives become

like waters and waste away

The Tall Building

Don't stand too long on a tall building
The view from the top may excite you
& so you suddenly forget the earth

For upon which every tall building stands
As man cannot walk the earth from the top
The dust underneath our fits are the earth
Remember that the top is for all men.

Knowing the shaking of the tall buildings
How mightily the echoes from its falls,
Don't live in the tall buildings in neglects

Of those along the way to the top too
Whose time and the ladder is on construct
Theirs might be of a golden metals &
Their land a gold mine of lifetime treasure

Don't stand too long on the tall building
The view from the top may excite you
& so you forget those mending theirs
The ladder to climb their tall buildings

In the crime of incendiary,

There was an egregious crime against us.
The black race of the world,
Our tears burn as conflagration!
& our properties destroyed.

As our tears thickened the cloud,
But there was no rain to quench it;
As our beloved cities and pride burns!

The arson against the black race
& the sins committed against us,
& the world sees no crime against it

Maybe for the world are theirs,
Of those who committed genocide,
Against the African continent.

When shall we forget that we died?
Not outside of our continent,
But we were killed and shipped
For the betterment of another,
But the world proclaimed us evil.

False Love

With the rush of fluids flowing down his body
& little space for which she could breathe from,
Those owl-like eyes she stared deeply at
As she is held underneath this giant monster
Thoughts run backwards to thousand times passed

The coming of this fellow who now is the beast
& the one underneath him she struggles for air
Because like the claws of an eagle against its preys
So he held her, & as the risen king held foes underneath,
Seeking for the dwellers of it overpowered folks to bowl,

Silence became the dark noonday of her visit
Tell me what it is, but you had made me believe it
& that men are the monsters in our world
They travel a thousand miles away from home
Seeking for what they do not have within &
When they get the key to the kingdoms

In might, they went in and let its gates plumb in asunder &
The kingdom becomes a wasteland of thorns
Where dwells brokenness and hatred for this gender
The one called boys.

Death Everywhere

Just like the other night

I heard cracking sounds,

My heart gallops like flames

Up like an inferno erupting

Maybe from a distance

Like an explosion of embers

As there emerge many lines

Of smouldering ray likes

The scars of the crack echoes

All on the other side our camp

As bodies became vapour like &

Just like an overheated kettle boils

As the inferno heat runs

All like the hurricane winds

The dreams of a thousand years

All vaporized into the tiny air, &

Forgotten by the ones we stood for

Is Life Made?

Who made life
And how has life being fair
Born in the remote village
Raised with leftovers
Clothed with rejects

Breaking the tick clouds
With this heavy metals
Of will and resilience
Unquenchable desires
Goals and aspirations

And there came a crack
At the persistence of will
To change the history
And retold the story
At our own sorry

But life knocked us off
& life has not been fair
To give us this thread
To ask, who made life
Because life has not been fair
As we battle blood pressure

My Tale As A Writer

Our lives are precious,
No doubt, but, can I live it with you?
A man's life is too fragile like air
Won't you give one a chance,
To live in the pages of paper?

They read our poems online
Journals and magazines
We are applauded for that
The acumen, wits and the craft
You are a good writer no doubt
Send us your works let's see

Tales of the upcoming writers
One word edited is equal to 4 naira
I have 60 thousand words
Check and balance the cost
What is your budget like
Call us when you are ready

You will pay for the proofread
The publication on soft and hardcopy
That amounts to small change they say,
We will edit your work to a standard

The worldwide book standards

Though you are an upcoming writer

This is a tale of an upcoming writer

Like a seed in a tree seeking life,

Seeing that there are wits in us

And that there is all it takes

To be heard across the globe

While not plant us in pages of paper

Like life in the seedlings are planted

That we will not sprout life and die off

Like seeds in a tree seeking life

And not like a writer without publication

Glover's Soldiers

O! Africa you must awake,
Arise from your many slumbers!
It is a decade and time has passed,
The hand that cuts itself deep
And rejoice in her own miseries

The Glover's slave men
The conqueror of her own land
The men who rejoice in brute
The harbingers of death at order

O! Africa you must awake
Arise from your weak slumber
Who is he that kills its own at will
And imagine to live in peace?
Africa arise from your sleep!

The Words On The Wall

There is a son born unto me
Who would have wished
To walk with me a long way
As his father and mentor

Even though it is just you
Like I had walked a long way
With my father in time past
But I don't know of our own

Read these words often time
To cheer yourself up within
For the journey is a long one
Fate knows why I fathered you

Let good parts fall in your way
To life, may you succeed son
And greater than I become
Mostly, may life treat you fairly

LIFE

Tell me if, yes,
if we are not like flies
Little time we perch on
We perch on lifelines
Our lives never last long
And our lives fly away
As our memories fly too
Into oblivious mists

And as we wonder,
If life was this small
Time and chance happens
Why do we occur this little
Maybe to shatter hearts
Or bring hopes and tears

In nutshells of existence
As nothing could sum up
Of our little existence here
Life is like flies that perches
And we perch to fly away

The Announcement

When he spoke those words,
I am not the man of tears
He never interpreted this
That even the heart pounds
More and bloods on pace
Causing the feared fate more

Now the announcement was,
John you are going to be on drugs
Your heart beats off ranges
This is called BP at your 30s
You need to start it fast as
Because it's a silent killer

The cranking walls fell off
Life of an earth man how short
With many unfulfilled dreams
Longings of the heart stares
The son I never fathered much
The daughter I had thought of
The wife I long to love till the end
And it heats the earth in might

And I Followed Unequivocally

And love found me
At the extreme sides of life
Where my vision became blurred

As it points its luminous rays
& I followed unequivocally
For there was this strength
Only true love could give
I felt within my being

It reassures of years wasted
In infatuation of a lover's heart
The renewing of once believed love tales

That when love founds a heart
It heals all its brokenness
& mend the bridge of the
Everlasting peace within
As one follows unequivocally

How I Became A Father

This was how I became a father,

At the first cockcrow

Mother would tap me

Wake up, wake up

This is the time real men wakes

They wake up to prepare

For the things, their wife would use

With the heavy shut eyes

I doze off again into a daydream

Where men are treated like gems

Precious in the hands of its holder

And not to be tapped at cockcrows

& 4 was the first tap

& 5 was the second tapping

Wake up to prepare for your siblings

What they will eat today after school

You are the first child, you live by example

Don't be too late and lazy to wake up

6 & 6:30 became a hard flog

& a knock, wake up as a man you are

Men wake up on time to prepare

Provide the things used by their wife,

Take up with you your knife and run,

Quickly to the farm and fetch firewood

This is how real men do early in the morning

Before the Sunsets they are already back

7 & 8, we are already nursing siblings

The ones left in our hands by life

Circumstances of life hit us hard at noon

& we became a father in brother's shades

For life has thought we learned well

As at our early days to become fathers

This was how I became a father

My Love

The equanimity I found
Over the life's journey
And the inner stability
Of genuine love you give
This I realized that love
Indeed is a tangible thing

Luscious and touching
Succulent oozing flame
Your presence titillate

Within me a partner
One that is to be called
A bone of my bone and
The flesh of my flesh as
We live together and

Forever as one body
Under the marriage
Allegiances and treaties

The Gulf Within Us

Look at the scars

The inscription of

Long ago squabbles

Out of what was ours

As we memorized lines

So not to be an outlaw

Prisoners of conscience

In our land, our voices are lost

The gulf within us is the scar

Our Fears At The Shore

So we waited at the shoreline

From where our voyage begins

There we saw the earth haze

As our visions became dim

But our hopes of tomorrow

This too kept us waiting for

After the wind, comes stillness

At first glance, the tempest-tossed

And the sailors encourage us

Saying, gawk not at the sea troubles

Think about the vision of your journey

The longings that you left home for

In search of the promised land

One across the sea flowing north

Over this troubled sea awaits you

Crowns of glory and lasting peace

That which seeks your inner man

When We Die Today

With all our thoughts,
Our clamoring to go
That abode of ecstasy

Out of inquisitiveness
We each day mirror it
What a moment to be

Breathe away from earth
And races into utopia
These are all with men

On this other side of ours
Who painted on us the
Heavens that we don't
Know what it looks like
In which we die living for

Have you been to heaven?
What are its dwellers like?
What fate awaits all there?

Those who painted it here,
On the walls of religion,
Have they been there before?

Whisper to them now, that

When we die today as man,

Will they paint our heavens?

An Old Man Seeks Rebrand

At the age of 66
    He has realized
        That name has
            Effects on him

        Bearer at will
      Nigeria was his
    Name glorified
With hard stones

Corruption his
    Symbols boldly
        Inscribed within
            The waving flag

        He is the killer
    Of what comes
    Out him as gene
And groans alas

In Our Hearts, We Say Farewell

Farewell my dearest warrior
Who died when death means
Nothing to the men of this end
And men who mourn not at death
Knowing that it strikes sudden

Your death at noon brings
With it a shadowless rays
From the noonday sun
As the heavens beckon
A judge for your innocence

Should you forget so soon
That death of this tent
Is not the death of the man within
Remember to rise to power
When he shall call your soul

Farewell my gentle soldier
You have lived once amongst us
Like the dove you bring tidings
The good news of the gospel of
Jesus Christ the savior of men
You shall forever live in our hearts

In our hearts, we say farewell

The Monsters You Made

A Poem Written after Burna-Boy' Monsters You Made

In retrospect,

What else could be told

Except for pains of mind

Our history with your men

The ones who sailed across

Atlantic oceans in an expedition

What else can be said,

If what we do today is evil

Your forefathers did it too

To our forefathers in dark

But we do ours with eyes open

Pains of the African child

The ones you once rejoice at

That it was mated to a people

Who welcomed you at ease

You conquered them in no war

Out of cheat and cunning ways

In the words of Burna boy,

We are the monsters you made

For your forefathers had once

Rejoiced over Africans shipped

Across the high Atlantic ocean

As means of developing Europe

Now our sons rejoice in kidnap

Dear God

A Poem Written After Dax's Dear God

Dear God, in the words of Dax

Why is it only you that children of men

has built so many religion for,

When from the Bible we read that,

God is not an author of confusion

But his creations have made him look like one

Dear God, the Jews said, they wrote the Bible

And all the Bible promises are their's alone

They saw God and he instructed them

Jesus Christ is for them and their offspring

And all the laws they try to keep to but

The coming, dying and resurrecting of

Christ Jesus some believe and others don't

Dear God why, the Gentiles claim that,

The Bible is written for them because,

The Jews were righteous already and need not

Of anything to make them right again with God

They embrace it with all their lives

The Jews see them as hypocrisy an

In turn, the Gentiles see the Jews as rejected

Dear God, why so many religions

Dear God, why so many things happening

Dear God, why do we run after shadows

In the quest to know you here and there

While your words and your ways are simple?

Who is the one to hold accountable for all these?

Dear God, the Romans said that you are theirs

They changed the Sabbath day to Sunday

And the Jews disagree with this and it resulted

Death as men and women of goodwill was

Eating up by hungry lions as the world watch

And the other isolate itself from the world

But daily it seeks to be the way to God

Another group emerged from the corner

The Bible now speaks of their religion

They are the chosen people of God

God's name is not just God but what they call

They forgot about their origin and ways

They fight to protect their religion not faith

Dear God, in the words of Dax,

Why do you allow so many religions?

Dear God, in the words of Dax,

Why do you allow multiple religions

To defraud your creations their rights to know you?

The naturalist sees you in all things created

And daily visit and reflects on them all

But the religious said you must be like us.

There is a great group of men,

They have seen all religions as one

And in one house lived to worship you

But the religious said, they are occult

Dear God, this sect and group of great men,

Their works are visible to the eyes of all

But their secrets upon secrets,

And their level upon levels breaks my heart

As none knows from where to dance from

In the words of Dax, why are there so many religions?

In My Country, We Are Wailers

In my country we are wailers,
We wail over our past chains.

The fathers told us it was evil
Ones did against their will

And yet day-to-day they run
After their once upon a time
Evil and embrace it with arms
Wide-open into obliviousness

As nostalgia for Africa ascends
Within their hearts of treachery
And everyone becomes a wailer

When the dice are not rolling
Either in their direction of affairs,
They wail and blame their fathers
Who died seeking a home with voice
That they failed to see within

When We First Met

When we first met
At the vestibule filled with white lilies
And she asked if I had brought her one

Yes, one amongst the beautiful flowers
That reminds her of true love she hoped for
For there is a hidden aura of pure love
Within the genuineness of nature & flowers

When we first met, she said
Take a good look at these beings
Are they not naturally beautiful?
With every part of them speaking
Love is natural like flowers

At Our Departure

They gathered and grieved
That if God could have saved you

Knowing from our standpoint
That you were an innocent man
Before the arrows that puncture
The air-filled balloons at noon

What does it mean to these sayings
A man born of a woman is of few days
Filled with wandering and troubles
The wages of sin is death in totality

But what becomes you the innocent,
You who we thought lived alright here
Is death the reward of benevolence?

Why do men die when they're needed
When life is in the middle of time
And dreams unfulfilled and stares at
The naked image of reality that we gaze at

Man dies and go and woman born
Another that will wait to die same ways
Let the voice be heard from every hill

That death is no more and humans live forever

MY ANCESTORS AVARICE

In their avarice to win favors

In the eyes of men from across the sea

They gave them our most valued possessions

Remembering not our dances at full moon

We became like birds without nests

African men and women

Shipped across the high Atlantic sea

The strength of the Fatherland forgotten

The gods silent and blind

In my ancestors' avarice to gain

Africans sold their future

And He Died

In fear and tears rolled
Permit him a passage
To the riverbanks of life
Where dwells serenity
And the shore current
Tells of the peace not
Humanly given at last
But heavenly paradise
As he lay down face
upward breathless

Let him find peace here
For many are the things
Most he had longed for
They stand and stares
At him and while he washes
Away from this earth life
Like though he hadn't been
Born for any good reason
Cold and as the frosts lay

Who would believe it,
That he was birthed here
When the birth was a necessity

But there arose a monster

Seeking to devour all there's

He left home in the morning

For a quest for which he is

Consumed as a young man

Racing within to find himself

As nothing else mattered to him

In the languages of rough hustle

He is seen lying down without

His dreams and visions coming to

Accomplished as he had thought it

For his life was cut short by shock

As a nation & a people,

We had desired to eat

the nuts of a kernel

Because we deserve it,

But the shell

of the kernel is

Hardened and

needs to be cracked

Our ego keeps us

away from it,

bending low

To crack

our kernels

At ease of heart

Because

we can't stand

In chaos and crack

Our kernel shells

while standing

We must learn

From the lower

To stand up tall

For the best is

Within us all here

As a nation & a people.

A Poem Dedicated To My Wife

The crown on your head

With its precious stones

Choice crystal & diamonds

Edifice of magnificence

In royalty and splendor

Dangling and glittering

Your beauty is my heaven

To dwell in your havens

Finding a resting abode

Within the shade of roses

Out of the chaos of life

This single act of love

Each day I seek in you

My wife and my best

Peace within the brooks

The equanimity I found

Though rivers of life flow

Up the hills and down again

Nothing again could be

Compare with your love

For I have found in you

My lost paradise on earth

For My Son Sobeife

14/05/2021

The joy of fatherhood,
What shall I liken you to?
Could it be like that oil,

The one that runs from
Aaron's head downward
Wetting his whole being

Words that are written
for our edification

Like those words spoken
From the mouth of Christ
That calmed the storms
And peace restored again
Within the troubled souls

The joy of fatherhood
It is beyond ephemeral
Everlasting is the euphoria
At the realisation of this

In the Bible book of Psalms
Chapter 133 verse 1, 2 and 3

As the dew of Hermon,

and as the dew that

descended upon the

mountains of Zion:

for there the LORD

commanded the blessing,

even life forevermore.

SOBEIFE and DADDY

For My Departed Beloved Mother

Mother

I am listening now from the thickened walls that demarcated my heart from the wailing of children

I heard the songs from the children who were living with their parents and I joined in like-minded now

Singing about their mother's day celebration songs

I have tried to be silent and learn diligently and muffled the voice for it not to be heard from the other side because I never knew what it was like to celebrate a mother's day in likes manners

You lived but a few days on the journey that was supposed to be built on eternity and endless memories of both faces of life here on earth

I am learning it now and it seems like the other way round, I mean the very hard way kind of

I've paid more attentiveness than I did last year and it amazed me how much I have learned to sing it now in the tune and manners it is worded

Sweet mother and sweet memories of your days with us all, day and night I wish you were here to hear me word those lyrics and to tell you how beautiful you are and have fought for us all

It's another Mothering Sunday, in like manners of the code 1005015 it has been repeated

I don't think it's a history to repeat but guess it is OK to be reminded of the uniqueness of the code in me.

Forgotten not your selfless love and sacrifice for your lovely children, I remembered you again

I love you so much and we love you so much and we hope we will see you soon and we will sing it together.

Broken Arrow

If you had known how fragile my heart is,
The orphan child who lost his only coin
Money given to him when life was tender
Beneath the inscription broken home,
You should have realized that his story
Is this one not to be told again to his own

Fragile hearts, they die every day unnoticed
In what you call retaliation and anger,
Ones that you cannot forgive in love,
Fragile hearts becomes like birds of air,
And they fly away from us in oblivion or,
They live half dead and in fears all lifetime

If the fragile hearts gets broken,
What becomes their way to see this life,
Deep pains pierce through them daily
As what they had seen as love and theirs
Is now that which is killing them unnoticed
Don't forget that fragile hearts cannot heal
They die in silence and go into oblivion of death

Friends Of Time

Friends of time

Years in number row

we count the stars

With our backs lay on

The ground we rolled out

Like rains in the skies

Falling to make mighty

Ocean on the earth surface

The paths we trod on

Friends of time

We stood hands round held

With fist pointing upwards

Gazing at the glittering moon

The wake of a new era echoes

We see the moon is older now

But our love withstood times

Friends of time

In the washing sand, we built

Our homes like memory lines

The abode we reside not in

Because it washed off on our wake

Trees we climbed together tells

Memories are to be a reminiscence

Friends of time

In time we wandered like

From whence the time goes

Like a push, it aimed at us

With just a push we launched in

Like strangers, we staggered

And time tells what becomes of us

Friends of time

In wars, we lay behind

Each other we fought with joy

Glancing at each other's face

The hope of victory in this battle assured

The realities of love surpassed wars

Lite the candle again tonight

Beam the rays of this light

Friends of time

When The Sudden Sun Set

In the solitude of my soul
That invisible core therein
I confide not with folks for life
And being that we are one
Fate, death, sand and grave
We comfort our hearts with
Words of encouragement

Since we live to die and die
To never to be remembered
In some cases remembered
We speak words to healing
Healing of our brokenness
That death is our reality then
How life has been unfair to us

Would you not come to me
Rather than conventional visit
To my graveside with flower
To lay it by the earth side of
My grave where I am not in
There to know what colour
Are your roses and the lilies

Death knocks harder than

Our life which is gently pressed

Into nothingness at the noon

When the sudden sunsets

And we are no more here

Love and words expressed at

The graveside becomes like

The birds of air and flies away

Oh, where is the sacredness

Of these my tears and the

Powers thereof in death?

Candlelight At The Graveyard

Tonight, we shall all matched
Into the graveyard unannounced
Every man with his candlelight
And every woman with her voice
To lite out the darkness of death
Out from the eyes of the infants
Those who died never seen the light

Every woman with her voice
To echo our grievance over death
The one that kills the unborn
And those who could not know
What the day's light is before they died
Tonight, we shall all match
Into the graveyard unannounced
As we light up their ways into the ether

Tonight, we shall at the top of our voices
Declare unto the East wind and West
To never come and flicker this light
From these souls who could not live
To see the beauty of life and light
As they return to the unseen world
And their little time shattered us all

The Eagle Fly Away

Under the shades of mighty iroko tree
I sit lately underneath to gaze
At the sudden phenomenon
Between the eyes that see
And the legs that carry the eyes

The two unicorns and the Eagle
It was not a hallucination at noon
As the eyes can't lead the way
And the legs are too weak to walk
I saw a nation with many flags

1960 the three cried out
Too long an enslavement peril
The cry for a nation of their own
Not rule and run by men across
The Seas of despotism and ill will

The Eagle in her great sight saw
A nation where agriculture rule
And the unicorns saddled with
The long walk to this promise
Landfill with mineral resources

But the unicorns ate up at will

A load of green agriculture
And Eagle decide to go blind
Under the iroko tree, I sit and
Watch over the events as it unfolds

As the Eagle fly away leaving
The two unicorns blinded by
Moving forward and backwards
Without a direction of where
To find their great eyes again
And there emerge Nigeria

A nation who lost her eyes to see
And her legs to walk her way into
Total freedom from neo-colonialism
Under the shades of an iroko tree
There I saw the Eagle fly away

This Other Side Of The Coin

I have seen it

The other side of the coin

Out of their niche

In the blood market

Where the nation's strength

Is sold out for personal gain

In camouflage of annihilation

The other side of it

There it is written bold,

Bring the youth into it

Brand them soldiers and

As the solution to our nation

Then sabotage their efforts

Until we have got all we want

The other side of the coin

Inscribe on it these words

Never will the youth rule

They are not qualified to

Bring them down to earth

By those, they are fighting for

Recruit them into our bands

As uniform men train them

Never to join the salvational

The outcry of their people at home

But be our peacekeepers

In the forest of no returns

The other side of the coin

You must not leave the office

To the one who is not despotic

One nepotism to another

The election is by our selection

And the people's choice is

Like the birds of the air

They must fly away from us

Dying Love

There was a time your portrait
Is on this wall end hang as
The most prestigious award
That I won your heart at last

Each night before my sleep
I would gait tiptoeing there
Having a gaze at the image
The only imprint you left off

The echoes of the night birds
And fears of your preference
Of wealth over true love sting
As the walls rheum in dust

The cracks at the spot where
You left the only remembrance
The choice portrait of yourself
They speak of your dying love

Poem To The Royal Family

Take him in,

To the temple

And lay him

There to rest

Away from

This world

We shall all

One day rest

With our face

Upward the

Skies so bright

As darkness

Disappears

Out from our

Ways to paradise

We shall sing

From the

Glorious hymns

SS AND A

The Duke is

Dead and

Another shall

Be born in

His place to

Serve as he

Has served

Lay him to rest

With the saints

To rise at the

Trumpet sounds

Of his savior

When he shall

Call the dead

In Christ will rise

Nameless Poem

If I should ascend
To the loftiest
Mountain cliff
To bring you
Roses, and lilies
As a sign of my
Love for you,

Of what becomes
Your heart seeing me
With those beings?

Love without a
Sacrifice is it love?

Complaints of the
Heart and murmur
These too kills love

If love is not sacrifice
Of what purpose do
We talk about it for?

Love without a
Sacrifice is it love?

107

Complaints of the

Heart and murmur

These too kills love.

Life Is Within My Heart

In this mist land
Vast is my dreams
As the road gets rough
And going gets tough
It looks like I am caught
On a lonely road of dreams

I kneel to take a look
At what is there written
In the tablets of my heart
For there lies the heaven
The first vision I behold
Before this journey afar

Into the frost and forest
I hobnob with nature
Looking not at that which is
Physical and terrifying
The stones are laid all

Down in the heart before
I have chosen to go on
Until I reach my heavens
Amidst this mist roads

Life is within my heart

Broken Muse Talks

If I could have grown wings
I would have loved to be
Like the mighty wind king
The bird of higher soars

Up to the site of the high hill
Hiding away from predators
Those that hunt me like folks
But foes in disguise killing

The little light of the day
The one they imagined
They seek to draw me
Down not soar as my call

If I could have been a bird
I would have loved to be
Likened to the eagle more
Phoenix to resurrect again

Because I am dying off
In silence and oblivion
Where darkness is light
And light is chased after

Marriage Hour

Unveil this veil
Tell me what it is
That you haven't
Said to me before
Yes I do I do

Unveil this veil
It has lingered
For many days and
Hours now hung
Till death do us part

Remembering our
Love like tender
Lilies that grows
By the river sides
Together forever
Until death do us part

Unveil this veil
Listening to the
Words of promises
And Vows we vowed

Men and angels

Bear us witness

Amen and amen

We are now one

AFTERLIFE

Blackness as the sands
And darkness is beauty
For it ushers in day light
I long to be dark skinned
Even in my afterlife

In my afterlife
I was amazed by the fact
That the angel who echoed
My name from the book of
Life was dark skinned

Different from what I am
Life afterlife with Africa
There is a hope for my
Black skin in the city of
Gold not made with hands

When this racist realm is over
Please wake me up in the
Eternal oblivion that I am
Still an African by the way
As God has made me afterlife

Tell him who sits at the seat

Of power that even in my

Afterlife, the township of

My town is as gentle as

The heaven rays upward

In my afterlife I am Africa

In my afterlife I am black

In my afterlife I am beauty

In my afterlife I am original

In my afterlife I represent earth

Help Me To Climb This Ladder

Help me to climb this ladder
I have had it written down
Within my subconscious core
That belief is all it takes as
To become who we desire

Help me to climb this ladder
The handwriting is written
Bold on the tablet of stones
Placed every corner I behold
That we are what we think
And thoughts made us thick

Help me to climb this ladder
Success in the heart is a push
Is needed to achieve greatness
As I strode this pathway along
Venturing into the unknown
With my eagerness just a push
I know where I am going if
You could lend me your push

Do Not Paint Me This Colour

Do not paint me this colour
Neither inscribes the name
The green that never prides
On its agricultural produces
But believes in the mercy of
Foreign plants, homelands
Lands laid waste out of fear

How could you possibly paint
White as the symbol of peace
And daily I am chaste angrily
By men on many uniforms as
Either an animal or a vermin
Ready to be annihilated with a
Weapon vomiting fire and I die
Raising the symbol they never
Honor as they preached to us
The national flag of this country

Do not paint me this colour
The land has seized being green
At the forest there emerges
Wailing of the men, women and
Children who went out to keep

The greener forest fit to feed us

Their blood flows and then red

Becomes the grasses and wail

Engulfed her whose name is

Nigeria and her colour green

and white turned horror even

In the eyes of the unborn child

WHEN I WILL BECOME

When I will become,
Like the birds of skies
I will grow wings strong,
Fly away with the winds
For there lies what I am

When I will become like,
Butterflies are hidden away
Underneath the cocoons
Amidst the earth's
Cacophony and din ears

When I will become like,
The shell that house nuts
Though needs a crack hits
Before its goodies are seen
As beautiful and appealing

Help me to find you within
You the still little voice in me
That whispers peace easing
Hearts that are entangled
From the chaos of earth
Nothing worth it voluntarily,

Kicking out that which I am not

Your Portrait

Hang it up there

It's an edifice to behold

Like the black diamond

It hanged on the wall end

Who crafted this one

It could be for a contest

With the goddesses

That you have taken time

To array yourself this way

Dangling on your neck

The precious stones lines up

Beads of choice gold

From the ancient world

You adorn yourself

Like the sun goddess

In the house of the gods

And the astronomers eyes

Seen the portrait hang on

Tonight give me a

Remembrance of you

The highest gift of all

Your portrait

Beautiful Souls Flies Away

Beautiful souls that flies away
From amongst us every day
Flies into the world of
 where dwells silence
Where we hear them no more.

But daily they live amongst us
From every leaflet turned over
Books and articles pen down

Like flicks of fire flakes flies
Ascending into the oblivion air
Where they join millions of stars
Up above the skies they stares
With their eyes dripping waters

At each one of us here groaning
But who knows what awaits us
For their parts they left halfway

Demons of death crunch on them
Less they stay to reawaken souls
Last night they came in legions
Holding them aback from moving
They lay down without a goodbye

122

As their beautiful souls flies away

I Am Finding Myself

I am finding myself
/ In this land of my birth
Where boys are not victims
/ Stories told one sided alas
That boys are load carriers
/ Children of circumstances
Born to carry their burdens
/ From off their shoulders

Into this land of no return
/ I bent over to tighten my shoes
For the long walks off this valleys
/ Stares at me like the skies above
Whispers of hope echoes within
/ a step forward lies the crown
I am finding myself

Bubbling in many colours
/ the thought races up and down
From where the heart is hidden
/ convinced that the future is sure
The walk away from illusions
/ illumination arise from within
Life at the last moment sweets

/ for I am finding myself

Is Religion Still Going The Same Way?

I came looking for you,

/religion.

The abode of the saints

/ in union

The gathering of brethren

/ in legion

At every nooks and crannies

/ in the region

Voices heard singing melodious

/ hymns

Prayer meetings held in households

/ fellowship of the brethren

Now I can't fathom the voices in oblivion

Is religion still going the same way?

Jesus presents as

/ the only way

Bible read all through

/ the sessions

Faith and faithfulness preached

/ faith with evidence shown

Names from the Bible

/ we are admonished with

Not on anyone's god

/ we were encouraged to call upon

But on the name of

/ Yahweh all day long

Is religion still going the same way?

The gathering of the brethren

/ in unison

Breaking of breads together

/ we read

Sharing in one another's plights

/ we are one another's keeper

The race not being for the swift

/ in grace we all run our race

Christ our pacesetter we're

/ encouraged

Is religion still going the same way?

Christianity,

How has Christianity not failed us?

when we go to the pulpits

To hear the words that uplifts

and fall inside dug pits

Where clergymen profits

Out from the bereaved

Hearts that long for healing

How does Christianity build us?

If It has not divided us more than it has built us

daily they tell their one-sided stories

That their creator hated his creation

Of their gods in white skins, black is evil

Who dwell in the constellations

And watches his images die away

As a loving creator who hates evil

Yet its servants dwell in nefarious

How has Christianity not failed us?

When we see their flaws, they say,

Leave it. It is in the hands of their gods

To judge, and to reward them of their sins

But when we sin, they rise and read

From their doctrines against our sins

How has Christianity not failed us

      When shall we return to love

   Leaving Christianity to embrace

      Emptiness and our souls stick

   Glued in love with work to show

When Christianity has failed us

  Learn to embrace love and compassion

My Bible My Compass

Forgive me my Bible
The compass of life
Where dwells confide
In a world full of chaos
How I have forgotten you
Lately I return to you now

When shall I rise again
Daily to look into you alas
Finding my way upward
For the fear of this earth
Looms and allure me off
The higher track of destiny

Into the bad land sinks life
Rising becomes illusions
The last breath lurks alas
Wishing and revisiting
Last walk through you
Reignite my dying soul
My Bible my compass

The gods, If They Are In Existence.

The gods in our frivolous perceptions of them,

has stricken us - with ignorance in our perceived cultures -

and left us more wounded in the hands of evil.

With strength we walked miles into the tip -

of the mountains, and the forest of wide animals -

plants, we have cuts the best trees and shrubs.

Making many images as craft of our hands,

and imagination of our hearts - but -

has not behold the gods - helping us

to drag the woods home.

With the same wood - our strength - and the craft,

we have - faction images - according to ourselves -

and bestowed them the name - gods - and we bow in ignorance
of our minds. -

With dirtiness of our hearts, we did eat ourselves, -

causing harms - to ourselves just because of ignorance

and we run to - the carved - woods and kneeling down,

we ignore our common sense and our ability -

to be gods in our own.

We sacrifice the best of our animals for the carved image,

with obliviousness of cleanliness to our environ & health;

we run worshipping what supposes to worship us, -

The gods, if they are in existence.

Our Wedding Pictures Were Flash Of Lights

How it all happened was like a man in a daydream,

the many wishes of the attendees to the event.

Post your styles and this is the best posture,

the ones we have selected from flash points.

The road is far from home, so, make it a memory,

to remember our journeys from the distance land.

This is our stories to tell those that are at home,

that we travelled from far away land for a wedding -

whose pictures were just a flash of light of cameras,

our memory of the wedding still lives with us,

As it could not live with pictures we posted to take,

and the camera man made us believe we were taking

real pictures and not just flash of camera lights.

The Owls' City

It was once called the city of owls, a city from where silence oozes at noon, and at night, its inhabitants' howls,

In an unknown tongue of hoots; just as their songs are in dirge; from the sorrows of their past: they assailed once their sorrows, hooting and hoping for joy, maybe the one from a distant future not seen.

It is called the city of owls, where its dwellers are drawn, in the Waterloos of many dreams, as their twilights are full of lament; and longings for memory, one they once call their own in joy, where oozing breeze never hurts them, those who are called by the name.

It is the land of fathers that lost in the morning, straying away from homes we once dance and play with our ancestors in flutes, where our mothers dance with their waist bent low to the ground, and the children playing at the full moon of our lands

Let Your Kingdom Come

With her voice, she whispered behind. // Let's make our kingdom come tonight, // And let's dwell in its home of ecstasy. // For kingdoms are not wild and woolly, // They are a garden well-tended to by all, // The kings, subjects, and all care for its peace. // Tonight, let's have a stroll down the seaside; // And be welcomed by a myriad of flowers, // Ones bearing our choices roses of many colors, // For all these twilight long, I have mended our cruise ship, // The captain and divers are ready to roll our ship, // Into the sparkling waters of devotion unreserved, // Where we will forever inhabit in peace of sanity, //Joy and tranquil, away from our noisy earth, // We will daily build and rebuilding our stories of love, // With the waters of the blue ocean as holy water, //From here we had set out our journey into eternity.

Spare Your Words For The Departed

If words that are said about the dead

                                       were to be stones;

the ones that are thrown at them

to cause more harm than death,

we would have become like the watchmen

                                       at every corner waiting; -

                                       maybe watching & waiting

against those who would not

                                       withstand your

                                       demons to resist them;

          Depression,

          Unfulfilled longings,

          Ill health,

          Family issues,

          we name but a few;

Those demons who appear in their

                                       regalia and in legions,

                                       echoing death!

                                     and without:

first;

second;

third and

fourth;

thoughts to throw; -

their heavy words

of condemnations

at your dying heart

that oozed.

For you had wanted to leave

this chaos you called out times, -

times without number and -

your demons rejoiced "at least; -

we now have a candidate -

for our filthy hands and omens",

now, take from the bottle;

half of the substance of death,

the one not meant for the humans -

consumption and then,

lay down and become like us;

to wander through the beyond.

If words were to be stone,

we would have loved to gather;

thousands of them for you;

laying them as bedrocks,

for you not to sink into

oblivious of darkness

Tongue Of An Orphan

This is another poem from where I am breaking my silence and musing in the tongues of an orphan child of the world, and this is to sing how we have cried as an orphan and never been heard from every thick wall that muffled our voices off the street of mercy and remembrance.

For it is a new poem that tells from where we have learned too quickly to shelter our desires with garments of voiceless wishes in the night, and how we are chased each day, by the breaking of the new day with the realities of the day, and who we are amongst the world today.

In this poem entitled tongue of an orphan, where we have muffled our desires with tears, and clothed our realities with coats of many colours we wore, from this refuge of the land we are born to; as to the sunrise, we arose to embrace life, with life's cracked-body too rough to be held with bare hands, but with wills, we embrace it with our eyes closed in rivers, as life has vowed to be life in all its forms;

For as an orphan child, we have learned to embrace embers of live coals with our bare hands, and as with thoughts and wills not to be burnt, we have thrown our fears overboard our ship to our dreamland, and are inventing the man next to us in the mirror of life's grief, and of one who has overcome the tsunamis of life's winds, and standing at the tip-top of the highest mountains; as we run this race in anticipation for a crown at last, though many are the life's blows and not like man's hits of fists against his fellow man, but, we have kept the dreams alive along the way to the crest, and for this is what life as an orphan child has been with us in the tongue of an orphan child.

And as we have been driven and drawn from life's springs, to water the land from where we are its survival of the fittest, for many are the dreams of our unquenchable desires, in this land of our journey to the promised land of all men, we have become of many troubles with good hopes, in the tongue of an orphan child dwells our tales of victory at last.

138

There Is A Good Day To Write About Our Memories

Yesterday, I took out the bottle of dye I found

under the bed in my grandmother's hut,

and I drew with it - a triangle on my heart.

In that triangle, I engraved the memories -

of my life as a pilgrim - who is a survival of

myriad of life's experiences as a child.

Outside this triangle, I wrote myriad of names,

some were those who - in my life on earth

have played one role or the other hand - alive or dead.

As I tried to limit the names for the next day to come,

for what I have written here is the beginning-in my heart,

it is what I can hold out today, as the triangle expands.

& as I held out my hands to draw on my heart,

it all became visible, the words of my grandmother,

she had once told me, there is a dye to write memories.

Out of my curiosity as a growing grandchild,

I visited her hut every cool evening with oozing winds,

and she would say, there is a good day to write memories

of those life has blessed us with - though they are not here,

this dye is specially meant to be used in writing in our hearts,
139

except for such moments, the dye stays hidden from the eyes.

I reached out my hands yesterday under her bed,

in that her small hut after many years of her death,

I am blessed to have found the dye for which I am using now -

To write about my memories with her,

our times together is what I am about to write here,

as it started from the gathering of clouds that rained.

ACKNOWLEDGEMENT

Although life has graced me with many wonderful souls on this journey, and pages of papers can't be enough inscribing your nomenclature here today but, I will try as much as I can to pen down many of you here as to show how I love and cherish our paths that crossed to each other's own.

Rev Father Kelvin (KC) Agbakolom, you are the umbrella on a windy day, you never allowed the downtrodden to be drenched by the heavy downpour of lives happening, thank you.

To the woman of my dreams, Ogechukwu Brigid Asuonye (Ezigbom) (Nwaanyi Oma) the Queen of my heart, dynasty and World. If not you, who else would have accepted me as a husband. Nne, I Love You.

To my wonderful children, Akalachi, Osinachi, Chinemerem, Chiawulamoke, Ifeamaka and to the strength of my youth and the heir to the throne of my kingdom, Chidebem Sobeife, you are all acknowledged here and, in my soul, deep down.

My beloved parents, Mr Onyeche Nathan Nwankwoala & Mrs Janet Nwauloaku Achonwa all of the blessed memory, I love you both.

Pastor Mrs Margaret Umukoro, "What you don't have, you can't give". Never despise the days of your little beginning, Mummy, your words are as precious as diamonds and thank you.

Mrs Joy Joseph Onyeche (Joy), how do I thank you enough for all did for me back then in the village after the death of our parents and our elder Sister Tochi. Joy, you stood as a mother to all of us, how can I forget such love just in a hurry, no, and never.

Tochi and Chinyere, I wish you both were still alive today, but I leave it to the Most High God.

Ikechi Samuel Onyeche, indeed you are a brother.

Ruth, you are my beloved last born and be blessed.

141

Mr & Mrs Tochukwu Amaefule, Mr & Mrs Ogiegba Alesei, Mr Sly ThankGod, Franklyn Abuchi, Uche Godwin, Promise Chiadikaobi, Onyebuch Promise N. To all of you out there, you are all acknowledged for the time life has given us to come to be brothers, sisters and friends, I am grateful for the opportunity.

Jude Thaddeus, Iwunze Obinna, Evans Nwachukwu, Napoleon Ikechi, Felix Ndidi, Aunty Miracle Anayo, Dr Festus Chioma, Daddy Godwin Asuonye, my brother/sister inlaws, you are in my heart as this work has come to be a reality, and I just want to say a big thank you for your support and encouragement through these years.

May we all live to see more of life's goodness now and always amen.

John Chinaka Onyeche "Rememberajc" is a husband, father, historian, poet and diplomat from Etche LGA of Rivers State Nigeria. He resides and writes from the city of Port Harcourt Rivers State, Nigeria. He is currently a student of History and Diplomatic Studies at Ignatius Ajuru University Of Education Port Harcourt Rivers State.

John or Apostle as he is fondly called by those who know him is an embodiment of literature and loves retention of African's original tales before the coming of the sea monsters, as ships and humans of the then known worlds.

His notable works are/can be found on the following websites:

Spillwords, Melbourne Culture Corner, Nnoko Stories, Tuna Fish Journal, Brittle Paper, Nymphs Publications, Youth Magazine, Acumen Poetry UK, Conceit Magazine, Mosi oa Tunya Literary Review, Rigorous, Open Door Poetry Magazine, Fever The Mind Magazine, Kalahari Review, Scars Publications Ethel Zine, and *Pangolin Review*.

John Chinaka can be reached through the following means:

Rememberajc.wordpress.com

Twitter.com/apostlejohnchin

Apostlejohnchinaka@gmail.com

https://linktr.ee/Rememberajc

Printed in Great Britain
by Amazon